MW01379614

The Story of Lynn

A mother's journey through love and loss

Patricia Smith

WestBow
PRESS
A DIVISION OF THOMAS NELSON

Copyright © 2012 Patricia Smith

All rights reserved. No part of this book may be used or reproduced by any means, graphic, electronic, or mechanical, including photocopying, recording, taping or by any information storage retrieval system without the written permission of the publisher except in the case of brief quotations embodied in critical articles and reviews.

ISBN: 978-1-4497-7205-5 (sc)
ISBN: 978-1-4497-7206-2 (e)
ISBN: 978-1-4497-7207-9 (hc)

Library of Congress Control Number: 2012919982

WestBow Press books may be ordered through booksellers or by contacting:

WestBow Press
A Division of Thomas Nelson
1663 Liberty Drive
Bloomington, IN 47403
www.westbowpress.com
1-(866) 928-1240

Because of the dynamic nature of the Internet, any web addresses or links contained in this book may have changed since publication and may no longer be valid. The views expressed in this work are solely those of the author and do not necessarily reflect the views of the publisher, and the publisher hereby disclaims any responsibility for them.

Any people depicted in stock imagery provided by Thinkstock are models, and such images are being used for illustrative purposes only.

Certain stock imagery © Thinkstock.

Scripture is from the HOLY BIBLE, King James Version

Printed in the United States of America

WestBow Press rev. date: 11/5/2012

To everything there is a season,
and a time and purpose under the heaven:
A time to be born, and a time to die;
Ecclesiastes 3:1,2

In loving Memory

I was inspired to write this book, by
the inspirational life she lived.

To my daughter, Lynn

Contents

Forward by Mary Ann Rodman	xi
Prologue by Sara	xiii
Preface	xv

Part One

Introduction	3
The Sunset Story	5
Chapter One ~ Lynn	7

Part Two

Chapter Two ~ December 18, 1984	39
Chapter Three - Your Life Can Change in a Heartbeat	41
Chapter Four ~ Preparation	45
Chapter Five ~ The "Firsts"	47
Chapter Six ~ Dealing With Loss	53
~ Lynn	53
~ Stephen	55
~ Paige	56
~ Wagon Spokes	60
~ The Jody Story	62
Chapter Seven ~ Reality	65
Chapter Eight ~ Tears	69
Chapter Nine ~ Gods Comfort	71
Chapter Ten ~ The Hole in My Heart	73

Chapter Eleven ~ Years Later	79
Acknowledgements	81
Epilogue	85

Forward
by Mary Ann Rodman

Lynn was one of a kind. Unique.

How unique? When her mother Patricia asked me to write this forward, I realized how short in Earth Time, our friendship was. Fourteen months.

How is it that a high school senior (and then college freshman) who I only knew for fourteen months, has had such an influence on my life? Not a day goes by that I don't think of Lynn, and what she might say or do in my place. Another little piece of math; Lynn passed from this earthly life over twenty five years ago, yet she is forever in my thoughts and heart.

Lynn had the gift of seeing past exteriors to the person within. With her sparkling eyes and infectious smile, you could not help but want to be her friend. When she looked at me, she did not see a newly minted, scared-to-death school librarian. Somehow, we connected in a way that happens rarely in life. I know Lynn considered me a friend; to me, she was the little sister I never had.

I believe Lynn's uniqueness came from the fact that *she*

knew who she was. She was strong-minded, strong-willed, and unswayed by peer opinion. She knew her place in the world, a rare thing in most of us, let alone a small- town Tennessee teenager. Lynn didn't so much march to a different drummer, but danced to her own tune. And what a lovely dance it was.

Lynn played the flute in the high school marching band. I once heard her play Van Morrison's beautiful *Moondance* as a solo piece. The song ends, begging for "just one more moondance with you." I imagine her in Heaven, waiting for the rest of us to arrive and join her in that joyous dance.

I, for one, cannot wait.

~ Mary Ann Rodman-2011

Prologue
by Sara

To say that Lynn was an extraordinary person is quite the understatement. Even as a child, she was one of the most complex and intriguing people I have ever known. She was dry and witty with a sense of humor that was unique. She had an attitude and a philosophy of life that many people would love to copy, including myself. Her wisdom far exceeded her young years, and her compassion for others was carefully guarded beneath an iron-willed strength. She was thoughtful and never forgot anything.

Lynn was, no doubt, a very special person. She blossomed overnight from a little girl in jeans and a "Dart Plastics" cap to a beautiful young woman who was the epitome of femininity in old lace, peach roses and baby's breath.

Lynn touched a great many lives just as she did mine.

I love her, and I'll never forget her.

~ Sara

1985

reprinted from the book *Roses in December*

Preface

Years ago I wrote a book, *Roses in December.* What began as a collection of recipes and memories, and Christmas stories evolved into a book that began my healing process. Many times I have been asked to share my book with parents who had lost a child. Each time I have done this I think these people are not reading this book to learn new recipes. They have lost a child. So this time I am just telling Lynn's story.

I wrote this book to share Lynn's memory, as well as my feelings about losing her. In no way do I intend to offer this as a self-help book. This book has been in my heart for several years. Now is the time to write it.

Part One

Introduction

She was supposed to arrive October 18. October 18 passed. Days went by. Weeks went by. I waited. And waited. All that time we had no idea if we would have a boy or a girl, no one did back then. Finally the time came. It was a very long day. At long last, our little girl arrived on November 5, 1965. She was beautiful, she was healthy and she was finally here. She was special. We named her Lynn. I don't remember her ever being late again.

The Sunset Story

Lynn was five years old, and we were driving home late one afternoon and we were facing the most beautiful sunset that one could ever imagine. Both of us consumed with the wonder, the beauty and all the colors. As we discussed this wonderful creation, Lynn began to repaint the sunset. She said, "If I were God, I would have put more purple on this side and a little more pink here and then maybe some yellow over there."

I said to her "Well Lynn, when you get to heaven, you can tell God how you would like Him to paint the sunsets."

She was quiet for a little while and then said to me "Mom, you will probably get there before I do, will you just tell Him for me?"

Chapter One ~ Lynn

Lynn was an easy child. From the beginning she was independent.

At three weeks old, she slept through the night. At nine months she gave up her bottle and never had need for another diaper after her first birthday. Many days she would sleep until noon and I would often check to see if she was still breathing. Of course she was, but I could not believe how easy this was to be a mother. Giving up the "passie" was not so easy, but we made it. I think I cried more than she did. She took her first step when she was one year old. It was a joy to watch our little girl grow, learning to walk and talk and develop her own personality. It was something new every day.

Lynn 's first playmate was Jana, (Lynn called her "LaLa" and Jana called her "Lynn Lynn"). They had their own language and we never knew what some of the words they used meant. Then, there were the twins Mark and Michelle, who lived behind us. Their pool is where Lynn learned to swim.

Lynn never cried when I would leave her with a babysitter. We often would need to be away on business trips, and if our parents were not available, she would stay with our dear friends Johnny and Dartha and their three children, DeDe, Monica and John. They spoiled her, loved her and treated her as their own. She was happy wherever she was.

Rarely did Lynn get in trouble. However, we had a white leather sofa and Lynn had a red ink pen. One day I came into the room to check on her as she played, and I could not believe my eyes. She was almost finished with her masterpiece on the sofa. This was not a dry erase pen.

I said to her in a rather severe tone of voice, "You sit right there and do not get up until I say you can". When I came back into the room she was right where I told her to stay and had completed her masterpiece with her hand behind her back. I had forgotten to take the red pen!!!

I remember when Lynn was about three years old and I found her going to the street on her tricycle and I said to her, "Where do you think you are going?"

"To my Papa's house" she quickly replied. He lived about three hours away.

She loved her Papa, and one reason was because the word

The Story of Lynn

"no" was not in his vocabulary. My father was a farmer and had big farm equipment. When we would go home for visits, the first thing Lynn asked was to ride on the combine. It did not matter how late or how tired he was, she always got the ride.

Lynn had a lot of her paternal genes that made her very direct and to the point. When she was three years old, our house was destroyed by fire. A few days later someone asked her if she had on a new dress and she said quite bluntly, "Everything I have is new."

Lynn's path of independence and direction blossomed. When she was about three and a half years old and sitting in her Daddy's lap she said to him "Daddy Bob, I need you to teach me how to do three things. I want learn to tie my shoes, learn to read and learn how to drive a car."

He said, "Okay".

The process began.

Lynn got her first puppy when she was about four years old. A black miniature dachshund. She named him Skedaddle. He was a really fun puppy and they played so well together. We took him to the vet for his routine shots. I asked them to give him a bath while he was there. That afternoon the vet called and said to me, "Mrs. Smith, I don't know how to tell you this...but your dog is dead!" I could not believe what I had heard, and I really did not know how to

~ 9 ~

tell Lynn. I took several deep breaths and tried to muster the courage to tell her. I thought, you simply tell her the truth.

Fighting back my own tears, I said "Lynn, we can't go get Skedaddle today."

She said, "Why not?"

I said, "Because he died."

She was quite for a few minutes and then said, "Oh well, we'll get a rabbit!

Beauty pageants were not for Lynn. I did convinced her to be in a Christmas pageant once. I dressed her in a simple navy dress. All the other little girls were dressed in frilly frocks. Lynn won. After the pageant, on the way home, I said to her,

"Lynn did you realize you won?"

She replied, "Yes and I was hoping I would!!!"

Later when I suggested she enter another beauty contest, she said, "Why I have already won!"

Her independence was demonstrated often as she was growing up. We entertained and enjoyed having friends over and Lynn did too. Her 1st grade teacher, Mrs. Luzelle shared with me that Lynn had invited her to come for a visit. She asked Lynn if she had discussed this with her Mother and Lynn replied "This is my house too!"

Lynn was an only child and it did not seem to bother her. She never talked about having a brother or sister. I

The Story of Lynn

guess she enjoyed the attention or the solitude. She was very independent and could entertain herself for hours. In her younger years, if she did misbehave I would send her to her room. Years later, she confessed to me that sending her to her room was like throwing her into the briar patch.

She loved her cousins and looked forward to her play dates with them. On one occasion, it was amusing to see her play with Mark and Tim. Lynn with her red cowboy boots, stuck in the mud, and all of them calling for help.

Our neighborhood was a great and safe place for children. If we had milk and chocolate chips cookies, then we could sleep late on Saturday mornings. The kids would watch cartoons until noon. If Lynn left the house before we got out of bed, she always left a note saying where she would be.

We built her a playhouse for her 6th birthday. Lynn's friends, Tammy, Yvette, Kelly and Denise had so much fun playing in that playhouse. Sometimes it was tea parties and who knows what else.

Our friends David and Nita lived across the street. David called Lynn " Puff" and she acted as if it made her mad. I think she really liked it especially when he would sing to her, "You are a cream puff". Dave, their son, was her idol. He was a little older, and she loved him. He had a great music collection that he shared with her. He made her feel special, especially when he would ride her in his dune buggy.

~ 11 ~

Lynn was a well- rounded young lady. She took piano lessons and swimming lessons. She won art contests and dog shows with blue ribbons. She loved Bible School and Sunday School. She was christened into the Methodist church as an infant. It was a very tender and humbling moment the day she walked down the aisle by herself in that same church and gave her life to Christ, at the age of 12. She had not discussed her decision with us. She allowed the Holy Spirit to direct her life.

Lynn loved music. She even wrote some songs with her friend Shane. There was always music in her room or in her car, but except for singing in church as a congregation, I could never get her to sing with me. Can you imagine how totally shocked I was the day she came home and announced "I am going to play the role of Lucy in the musical *You're A Good Man Charlie Brown*. A leading role? Singing? Together with her friend Sharon, Shane, Jamie, and others, they made great memories with that musical.

She developed her own sense of style very early. I enjoyed sewing and creating clothes for her. It soon became apparent that she had her own ideas. A pair of old sneakers with no strings and a red "Dart Plastics" cap was her signature for several years. The ball caps were later traded for hats and she wore them with confidence.

She would remark, "A hat says you have the confidence to

The Story of Lynn

wear one!" And I heard her say many times "To wear a hat, all it takes is guts." Lynn collected vintage handkerchiefs and always had one tucked in her sleeve or in her well organized purse. She also enjoyed wearing vintage clothing. For her junior prom, she decided to wear a dress that my mother had sewn for me when I was 15-years-old. A pink silk organza over satin creation. It fit her perfectly. She was beautiful and I never saw her happier in any other fashion. She was invited to a party on short notice, and told me that she needed a long dress for the occasion. The night before, we found some voile curtains and with her lace blouse, together we created her "Scarlett" dress"

She had many thoughts about fashion and even wrote them on little notes. A few "Lynnisims"

"Fashion doesn't mean style." (Fashion is a current fad designers are pushing, style is individual and is never affected by fads")

"Never buy a maybe!"

"When its right, nobody has to tell you!"

As she got older her independence and self discipline became more obvious. We never had to wake her. She had her own time frame and her own schedule. On the closet door in her room, Lynn kept a calendar with dates and events a year at a time. She remembered her friends and family with cards or a note. She had a schedule and always stuck to it.

She did not like to be late. She would say to her dad, "It is time to go the ball game!"

He would say "But Lynn, the game doesn't start until seven."

She would reply "But Dad, they run out at 20 'til".

Lynn's grandmother owned a ladies apparel shoppe. Mildred's on Main Street. We all worked there, my mother, my sister, Lynn and I. Monday was the day to "change the windows". What a treat for us when Lynn began to assist. She mastered this with her own abilities and involvement. She was 14, and this became a part time job for her. She took this responsibility seriously. If she had other plans on her days to do the displays, she arranged her schedule in order to accomplish the task, even if it meant getting up at 5 AM.

She was very good. I have vivid memories of many of the window displays she created. She even kept a portfolio with the pictures of some of her designs. She thought they might come in handy for a job interview someday. One autumn for back to school, she dressed the mannequins in cords, plaids and the latest trend which was knickers. We thought she had finished and that she had gone home. Later she came back with big garbage bags full of beautiful leaves and filled the window with them. It was spectacular. Lynn always had a way of putting on that finishing touch. We called her our silent salesman.

The Story of Lynn

Scott, her close friend and fashion icon as well, would come in the evenings to help and support her. The mannequins were old and dated and Lynn really wanted to buy a new one. They were very expensive but her Mama Mil finally said yes, and we were off to market. The one she selected had a big blonde curly wig. Lynn named her Opal (from the daytime soap operas). Opal was like a member of our family. Our customers knew her by name.

We heard her night prayers always. She would call to us and say "Coming up to hear night prayers?" We wondered how long this would continue. She was 14 and still called to us, "Are y'all coming to hear night prayers?" She "God blessed" almost everyone including all the dogs we ever had. One night we looked at each other and realized she had not called for us to "come up". We knew she was growing up.

Lynn was not afraid of much. There were two things, however, that terrified her; mice and thunder. One day I came home to find her sitting on the kitchen counter. I asked, "What on earth are you doing up there?"

"I saw a mouse", she said. She had been sitting up there for almost two hours.

At night, if there was thunder, you could expect her, like clockwork, to be down in a split second and get into our bed. There was never a word spoken and this continued as long as she lived at home.

Bob bought an antique car, a 1949 red Ford that he completely restored. He thought it was fine and that Lynn might enjoy driving it someday. She would have no part of it, so we put it in storage. Later we considered selling it. She came in one afternoon and asked, "What happened to the old red car?"

"In storage," I said.

The old red Ford came out of storage, became known as Eunice, and Lynn loved her. With a standard transmission that many of her friends could not manage, she took right to it. Her friends tell so many stories about Eunice and how many of them could get in the car at one time. In those days, no one worried about seatbelts. On one occasion I asked her to drop me by the shop. We backed out of the garage and Eunice stopped. Lynn got out of the car, raised the hood, put the stick under to hold the hood up and did something. When she got back in the car I asked, "How did you know how to do that?"

She replied, "Do what?"

I was amazed. After a few years, Eunice had served her purpose, and we went car shopping. Lynn's dad told her that she could get a lot more car for the money if she left off some of the bells and whistles.

She said to him "But Dad, I have never had a car with bells and whistles." Consequently, Lynn drove her new Mazda out of the showroom as happy as could be.

The Story of Lynn

Lynn was very sensitive to others. She remembered how it felt to be dependent on someone else for a ride. She tried to include those friends who were younger when going to the movies or a game, especially Sonya, Lisa, and B.K.

Lynn was full of surprises. It was quite a shock to me the day she came home from school and said, "Mom what do you think about an exchange student living with us for a year?"

Well, I did not think that was something that I wanted to do.

I said "We will discuss it with your Dad." I am sure she already had a plan and would figure out the way to get it done. The three of us discussed it and took a family vote. Lynn and Bob won. We looked at pictures and profiles and decided on Anna from Sweden.

Anna's interest included cooking, gardening and playing the piano, three things I especially enjoyed. I thought," this could be fun". As it turned out, Anna did not have much time for those interests. Anna was 17, gorgeous and would not be able to drive in this country. This would be a challenge for me. Although the schedules did not always match, we made it work. It proved to be a wonderful experience for Lynn and also for us. They got along quite well. One time I do remember a bit of a problem. Anna parents had sent her some caviar in a tube, and Anna chose to have it for breakfast. Lynn had to leave the room.

~ 17 ~

The two girls learned a lot from each other. Lynn spoke with a Swedish accent and Anna developed a southern drawl. It proved to be a very fun year.

When the year was over and time for her to return to Sweden, Lynn made Anna a scrapbook of her year in America. One could see Lynn's sense of humor as she captioned under one of the of the pictures in front of the Magic Kingdom at Disney world "Our Summer House"! It was truly a great year.

Coleman was Lynn's paternal grandfather. Lynn called him "Coleman" because when we asked him what he would like for us to teach her, he said "Coleman, that's my name". Coleman had a pool table and Lynn loved playing. She also liked to win. She and her cousin B.K. learned to play pool together.

I did not give much thought that shooting pool was anything more than a pastime. Anna came home one afternoon and asked if we were going to the pool tournament. She said Lynn was competing and not just with her own age group. I think they were pool hustlers. She won several tournaments and money, too, I think! Her dad was mighty proud, and he bought her, her own custom pool cue.

Lynn was very creative. She always enjoyed drawing and coloring. When she was quite young, she did a watercolor of a mushroom for my Christmas present. She asked her Papa

The Story of Lynn

to take her shopping for a frame. It is still one of my favorite gifts, it hangs over my computer.

Lynn loved Christmas. We had tree trimming parties, and on the last day of school before the Christmas holidays, Lynn and her friends Tammy, Lanetta, Terri Li, Sonja and Maurica looked forward to having their annual lunch together. Our Christmas Eve tradition was dinner and gifts at my parents. My sister and I always tried to find the best present for each other. One year was really special for me. Sara had found my last doll "Saucy Walker" from childhood and had it restored. Lynn and Sara together figured out that Saucy's original dress was in Lynn's doll clothes collection. They could not wait for me to open the beautifully wrapped doll. Everyone was in tears. Joey, Lynn's boyfriend that year, went home, and his mom asked "Did you have fun"?

He replied, "Patricia got an old worn out doll and everyone cried!"

I believe that one of the most awesome responsibilities that we are given is being a parent. I heard Bob tell Lynn many times "I always want to say yes to you when you ask, but if I say no, it is because I love you."

It was the week after Christmas, and the Baptist church had planned a trip to the mountains. Lynn and Joey were planning to go. All the bags were packed and everyone was so excited. On the morning they were supposed to leave, we got up very early and were surprised by a winter storm. I assumed the trip was off. The weather channels and the highway department were saying to stay off the highways unless it was an emergency. We talked back and forth with other parents, highway officials and the youth leaders. Our feeling was that the trip should be canceled, but that was not our decision to make. But it was our decision for Lynn. She was not going. It was so hard to say no. It broke my heart. We were the adults and we did what we thought was the right thing to do. Since Lynn could not go, Joey didn't go either.

The others left on the icy roads and by night fall (before cell phones) there was no communication. Since the road conditions were so bad, the group had to spend the night in a gymnasium. I am sure the youth had a wonderful time. Lynn was miserable and so was I. As a parent, one must do what one feels is the right thing. We never second guessed our decision.

Cooking is one of my passions. It was not one of hers. One summer, I suggested it was time for her to learn to cook.

She told me," I can read a recipe and follow it, so don't worry."

Pizza and grilled cheese were two of her favorites and I didn't have a recipe for either. However, she could set a fine table. Often I would come home from work and find the table set in style. I never had to tell her. She accepted

The Story of Lynn

responsibility. She had such a flare. Even if we were having canned soup and grilled cheese, we dined in style.

After her graduation trip to Hawaii, she had a fun summer. She enjoyed sleeping late but would leave notes if anyone called for her (especially males) to wake her.

We began to make plans for her to enroll at Lambuth University. She planned, we shopped, and we packed. Anticipation mounted. The summer passed so quickly. It was time. Lynn was off to college to pursue a career in fashion merchandising. She was so excited and ready to embrace the world.

At Lambuth, she maintained her independence. I also attended Lambuth and when she was involved in sorority rush, she was concerned that I would be upset if she did not choose my sorority. I assured her that I knew she would make the right decision. She chose to go with Phi Mu instead of my sorority. She was beautiful in her white Battenburg lace dress for the pledge service. She wrote her dad and me the most beautiful letter to thank us for allowing her to be a part of such a wonderful group of young women. Here is what she wrote.

Patricia Smith

Dec. 3

Dear Mom and Dad,

Last night, Phi Mu had a special meeting about finances. As initiation gets closer, many of my pledge sisters are really struggling to pay their bills. The meeting was basically a "rap session" of the actives telling how they had similar problems and how they cut back, etc. Some said they had never really sacrificed money but time instead. Others told of how much Phi Mu meant to them and that even if dues were $100 a month, they would find the money somewhere.

One girl said, to this day (she's a senior), her parents don't understand why she sacrifices so much for Phi Mu. Another said her parents couldn't believe what Phi Mu has done for her – she's more outgoing, etc. Nearly everyone cried. You I could feel the genuine love everyone has for each other.

I just wanted to write and say thanks for making it possible for me to be a part of Phi Mu. I realize it's a big investment but those 40 girls bring me joy (Dad's word!) every day. I can see already what a special

bond is forming. I think Phi
Mu will strengthen me and help
me to become a better person and
hopefully, you'll see this and
know the money was worth it.

I also want to thank you
for my more-than-plentiful
checking account. I try to watch
my spending but I often splurge
on a pizza (or two)! I know
many people my age don't have
near the advantages I do and
I'm very grateful to you both
for making them possible.

I also realize many people

The Story of Lynn

don't have parents like I do.[7]
A girl in Phi Mu is not only
putting herself through college but
this Christmas, she's having to
pay for her own wedding. Her
Mom sent her $100.

I want you both to know
I <u>love</u> you very much and I
appreciate all the things you
do for me. I miss you a lot!
Thanks again for everything!!

☺ Lynn

P.S. See! Not all letters from college kids
say, "Please send more money!"

Patricia Smith

She invited some of them to our annual Christmas tree trimming party. She called and said "Mom don't forget to make the candy strawberries."

Lynn's first semester was going great.

Lynn's First Valentine

Lynn as an Infant

Lynn Waiting for Santa

Lynn & Tric

The Story of Lynn

Lynn Thanking Daddy for Playhouse

Lynn and the Puppies

Lynn & Tammy

**Lynn and Friends Christmas Lunch
Sonja, Lanetta, Lynn, Tammy, Maurica and Terri Li**

The Story of Lynn

Lynn & Her Scarlett Dress

Lynn Ready for the Prom in My Dress

Patricia Smith

Opal

Opal

Lynn at Mildred's

The Story of Lynn

**Lynn & Scotty
"Best Dressed"**

**Lynn & Her
Red Pumps**

Me, Lynn & Anna at Disney World

Lynn and Favorite Food

'Charlie Brown' Cast

The Story of Lynn

Graduation Night

Graduation

Lynn & Eunice

Graduation

Lynn Off to Hawaii

Part Two

Chapter Two ~ December 18, 1984

The day was December 18, 1984, a cold rainy afternoon. Lynn, a freshman at Lambuth University, was on her way home for the Christmas holidays. I was at the shop. We were all looking forward to her enthusiasm, her excitement, the tales she would have about school and her new friends. We heard the sirens, but you hear them a lot on Main Street. Then the rescue squad came in the shop, and said it was Lynn. I should go to the hospital.

I asked, " Is it bad?"

They said " Yes."

As we headed for the hospital, we came upon the ambulance, and I said," It is not going fast".

No one ever told me. I did not ask. I knew. I simply knew.

They did tell me that it was about 2 miles outside of town. There were two 18 wheelers. I knew then that Lynn "got there" before I did.

Chapter Three - Your Life Can Change in a Heartbeat

I remember that December afternoon just like it was yesterday. I remember where I was, what I was wearing, who said what and who tried to tell me where to go and what I should do. I just sat outside the hospital in the cold December air and waited for Bob to come and take me home. My little girl was gone.

We went home. Our family and friends came. They embraced us. They hugged us. They brought food. I could not eat. I just walked around. There was nothing anyone could do. My life had changed forever.

They told me my Uncle Dan was one of the first to arrive on the scene of the accident. They told me her things, almost everything that had been in her dorm room, were scattered on the pavement and in the mud. Some of her jewelry was found. They put her things in our basement to dry.

The next few days were filled with friends and food, calls and visits, cards and flowers. So many wonderful phone calls. Helen from Starkville, who had given Lynn all the Dachshunds, called, and we cried together. Sandy my friend and Lynn's as well call and we reflected on the wedding that we had dreamed of for her that would never be. My sister was in Nashville and arrived in Adamsville before I could blink.

Some would say I was probably in shock. I was shocked, but not "in shock". I did not take, nor did I need any medication to help me "get through". I needed my wits and strength to get through the next few days.

The next morning, we had to begin to make arrangements for the service. Bob and I prayed together as we always had. It helped us to face the day. Of course, we wanted it to be a celebration of Lynn's life. I wore red. The jacket was also Lynn's favorite. There were so many decisions. Visitation, where will the service be, the music, a coffin, a cemetery and then, you want me to put her in the ground?

We did the best we could. We had not had any previous experience. I know it is only the body that we bury and that her spirit will live forever but this was my little girl. I did what I had to do.

The church was filled to overflowing with family, friends and flowers. The music was beautiful. Billy Joe sang The *Rose*,

Stace and Shane played their trumpets, *Precious Memories*, and Lynn's Phi Mu sisters filled the choir and sang *Friends*. The congregation finished with *Love Divine all Love's Excelling* which was one of her favorite hymns. Then to the cemetery, as difficult as that was, I believe that was the easy part. The hard part was yet to come.

Living without her.

Chapter Four ~ Preparation

As I reflect on the time before Lynn's accident, I believe that God was preparing me for her death, even though I was not aware of it at the time. My father and I were making our annual Christmas shopping trip. We called and asked Lynn to have lunch with us. On the way to meet her, we passed a monument sales store and I remember thinking "what would I select if I were to need one for Lynn?"

Lynn came home the weekend before the accident. She was so excited about some new music. We sat on the bed and listened together. One of the songs was *Friends* by Michael W. Smith. The words... "friends are friends forever"...Its hard to let you go... in the Father's hands"...There just were little signs. I look back at these small signs.

It seems now that God was preparing me.

Chapter Five ~ The "Firsts"

Then there were the "First". All the occasions that come around after the loss of a loved one: the first week, month, year, first birthday, all the holidays. We were in the throes of Christmas, when the accident happened. The tree was decorated, the presents wrapped. There was the Christmas cantata at our church. Bob and I had practiced it for weeks. Could we do it? We decided to try, and we did make it through.

Then Christmas Eve, O my! What a fun time that had always been, but now! We still had to think about my sister's children. Elizabeth and Stephen. We had to make the best of it and get through it for the little ones. Traditionally we had celebrated Christmas Eve with my family at my parents' house. Instead we decided to have all the family, Mom Mil and Pop, Mike and Sara and Stephen and Elizabeth stay at our house. We knew Santa would find his way. The empty

~ 47 ~

chair at the dinner table stared at us. As we opened our gifts, the ones for Lynn were so obvious. What to do with them. We opened the ones from Lynn to each of us. Lynn had bought for me a beautiful peach silk lingerie bag. Sara gave me the gift she had for Lynn. Beautiful, feminine insulated underwear.

Just after Christmas we were invited to a wedding. Should we go? Did we want to celebrate? I did not want the other guests thinking about our grief. These were our friends and their daughter. We did go to Yvette's wedding. I am so glad we did.

A few weeks later, Kelly celebrated his Bar Mitzvah. Of course, we had to go. We had watched Kelly grow up and Marty, his dad, had been our friend for years. The celebrations of life happen only once.

January 15, 1985 was a FIRST. A memorial service for Lynn at Lambuth. It was a beautiful service. Her roommate Debbie and her Phi Mu big sister, Sally shared words of appreciation. That day was one of the easy ones. I know there were many praying for us. This is the prayer that was offered that day.

Almighty God, our Father, from whom we come and unto whom we return, and in whose care we constantly are, You have been our dwelling place in all generations. You are our refuge and strength, a very present help in time of trouble. Be with us now as we pray,

The Story of Lynn

and grant us Your blessing in this hour. Enable us to put our trust in You that our spirits may be calmed and our hearts comforted. Lift our eyes beyond the shadows of earth, and enable us to see the light of eternity. We ask in Your name. Amen

Then we had to go to her dorm room and pack her remaining things. That was not an easy task.

~ The First Valentine's Day

Both being romantics, Lynn and I loved Valentine's, as did her dad. Valentines Day was special. As a child, Lynn would make me a valentine, draw a picture with a poem and always write "I love you, Mom". That was a tough first.

~ The First Easter

We celebrated Easter, first by going to church together and later for lunch and egg hunts. Lynn and I usually had a new hat. Her Easter basket still reminds me of her anticipation of the goodies she would find and also, of the boiled eggs I would find weeks later under the sofa. That first Easter we went to church and I wore a hat

~ The First Mother's Day

Mother's Day is especially hard. I still do not attend church on Mothers Day. It is really hard to say why. I just can't, or I don't. Bob and I stay at home and cook for our family and friends. We honor my mother, the mothers in our family and the mothers of some of our friends.

~ 49 ~

~ The First Birthday

November 5, Lynn's birthday. Our family has always celebrated birthdays in a big way. My mother believed that this should be your own special day and she made it happen. Lynn's favorite cake was a coconut cake and I made it every year for her. I decided that I would try to do something for others to keep this day positive. My friend Sandy and Lynn shared the same birthday. One summer, Sandy survived a swimming pool accident with a broken neck. As a treat for her and myself, I invited all her sisters and some friends for lunch. The pressure was on for the table decorations. Bob blessed our food with the most beautiful prayer and we all cried. That is a memory that still makes me happy.

Lynn's Birthday Cake

1 box white cake mix	1 8oz sour cream
½ cup oil	3 eggs
1 can (8½ oz) cream of coconut	

Mix all ingredients with mixer. Bake in greased 12x20 pan for 30 minutes at 350

Icing

8 oz cream cheese	1 tblsp milk
1pkg frozen coconut, thawed	1 box xxx sugar
1 tsp vanilla	

Blend powdered sugar with softened cream cheese then mix milk and vanilla. Spread over warm cake and sprinkle with coconut.

The Story of Lynn

~ The First Thanksgiving

Our friends, Margaret and Benard invited us to join them on their boat for Thanksgiving. Although each FIRST had been difficult, we really had a good time that year in Naples, Florida. We all rode bicycles to church. It was a quaint little church beside the water and the service was outside. Sometimes a change is refreshing and healing.

~The First Anniversary of Her Accident

December 18th. Bob and I spent the day together. We continue to do something together each year. We always visit the cemetery and carry fresh roses.

~ The First Christmas

The Christmas season is still very difficult. We are sometimes invited to parties. There are parades, cantatas and many other holiday activities. Sometimes we go and sometime we don't. Sometimes we entertain, and sometimes we don't. Each year as I unwrap the ornaments that Lynn had given me or the ones she had made, tears well up, and there is a lump in my throat and memories overwhelm me. I, sometimes get a little carried away with decorating although it took me a few years to be able to decorate at all.

Each year around the first of November, I bristle up. I get a grip. I try to hold on until the anniversaries begin again.

Chapter Six ~ Dealing With Loss

Dealing with the loss of a loved one is so personal. I believe that one must do whatever it takes to survive. Bob and I prayed for Lynn every day. I never blamed God nor did I ask why. We prayed for her safety and for God to watch over her. I believe that he did, but it was her time. It was not the time for me to let her go but it was her time. I had to accept it. There are many stories that I could share of situations that have happened and how others have dealt with their loss. Each of us has our own way.

~ Lynn

Lynn named her second puppy Tric. Although Tric was a housedog, he got out one day and ran across the street. The German Shepherds he encountered were more than he could handle. I cried and cried and cried. Lynn was silent. She found her paper and crayons and drew a picture and wrote, "Tric we love you...you have to die sometime."

Patricia Smith

~ Stephen

Stephen is my nephew. He was seven years old at the time of Lynn's accident. A quiet child by nature, he made crosses (book marks) and drew "Lynn and God". "God and Lynn".

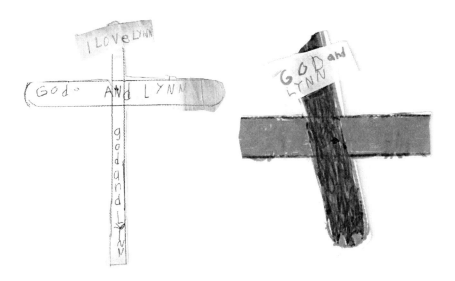

~ Paige

Paige was a good friend of Lynn's in high school and it was a bittersweet surprise to read her thoughts in the school paper the following year on Lynn's birthday.

Happy Birthday, Lynn. I know that of all the wonderful birthdays you spent during your brief life here on earth, you have never celebrated like you are celebrating now. This November 5 must have seen the most jubilant party ever. I know this, Lynn, because you're spending this birthday in heaven. surrounded by splendors this world could never begin to offer. Still as you birthday comes around again, your 20th now, there's a big part of it missing. You.

Everyone that knew you, and some that didn't, miss you. After you were gone, one of the most spoken phrases was, "She was the most 'alive' person I ever knew."

I guess it is true what they say about not noticing someone until they are gone. I never told you but you had one of the most natural smiles in the world. I wasn't the only one who thought so, either. Everyone is saying now that there was hardly ever a moment when you weren't smiling--you seemed to almost bubble.

Of course you had your moments as did everyone else, when something or someone else made you unbearably mad. Remember your senior group band picture for the annual? "G-R-R!" was under the picture after you signed my book.

The Story of Lynn

You always seemed to make people feel comfortable around you-whether you really knew them or not Your constant smile and sharp sense of humor revealed a kind heart beneath your person. I guess what people in general remember most about you is, of course, your impeccable taste and flair for fashion. You would love today's things and we could really use your guidance as the standard again.

I know all this seems to lean toward the "stream of consciousness" style of writing but there is so much I would like to tell you. so much to catch up on. So little time...

I remember that Tuesday last December like it was yesterday. It is still hard to think about it without shedding a tear. It is hard for me as I write this column for you.

Anyway, it was cold and rainy: and I was lying around the house as usual. The phone rang; and a special friend of mine told me about you before my dad could tell me in person. I was in shock. I could hardly breathe.

I got dressed somehow and daddy took me to Lanetta's house where I fell into her Mother's arms and cried. Lanetta was brought home from work shortly thereafter, and we held each other and cried. A little later. Tammy came over, and the three of us cried together. For hours we sat and talked about the wonderful memories we'd each shared with you. None of us could believe you could be gone.

Later Tuesday, I went to Sharon's house. I felt as though everyone had forgotten her. She just sat and stared. We sat in her den and talked about you. We laughed as we would imagine you looking down with your "signature" looks and saying, "What is this girls?!" I know ya'll aren't crying!. You had the most notorious looks and expressions, Lynn.

I, too, have several memories of you. I have the cutest picture of the two of us at the city's centennial. all dressed up in bonnets and bloomer. Did I ever show it to you? Remember the year there were six of us girls in one room in Gatlinburg? What a weekend. And who could forget the last weekend we spent together? Sharon, B.K. and I went to Lambuth to see you. You met us in the yard as we drove up. smiling of course. You showed us around.

Some newly graduated friends might try to look like real "big shots" or older to look impressive to the other college people, but not you, Lynn. You never once made me feel in the way, or like "your little tenth-grader friend", or unimportant in any way. You also helped me out when I practically broke my ankle running across campus. You also went across campus to get me an Ace bandage so I could walk--without being asked. You just thought it would make me feel better, and did it. You were really a true friend of mine.

One particular incident I would like to share with you and everyone reading this message is about the time I was at

The Story of Lynn

your house after Christmas last year. Your parents had gone out of town on a trip and other members of your family were watching the house. Mark and I were there building fires in the fireplaces and checking the pipes when I felt compelled to go upstairs. I has never been upstairs to your room before, but I had always wondered what it was like. As I walked up the stairs, I felt drawn to your room. I only made it to the door. I stood there, looking in, and an emotional force was present, so strong that I felt it warm all over. The presence was so real and so intense I was actually afraid. I started to cry as I finally got the courage to walk inside. As I walked around and viewed the items there I got to know you all over again. There is truly only one Lora Lynn Smith and you will always be here with us, just as you were there to meet me that day.

As I sit here at my desk, I wonder if you already know all these things I'm telling you. I wonder if you know how we feel about you. I hope you do. I hope you know we miss you and that we love you. Still I wish I had told you what a great friend you were...

To the students

It hurts so much to lose a friend or loved one. Through the past few years, there have been more than a few young people killed, consequently, several friends have felt and continue to feel great losses. Friends are priceless and good,

~ 59 ~

true friendship is sometimes hard to come by. Don't let yourself go through life without experiencing the joys of friendship.

It might be hard to reach out after losing a close friend. I know. But do reach out. Be a friend and you will acquire friends. And most important of all--let your friends know how you feel. This does not mean hugging them every time you see them or even telling them you love them every day. You can show friendship and love in simple ways. But however you show your love, admiration, respect, or happiness, make sure you do show it, Share yourself as Lynn Shared herself.

And Lynn, we'll miss you and we'll remember you forever. You were a great example for all of us. We wish you the" happiest birthday ever"...and we know in our hearts you have already gotten it. We love you Lynn.

~ Wagon Spokes

Our shop was just across the street from the local newspaper. Bill, the owner and editor, had watched Lynn grow up and watched her dress the windows at the shop for several years. They shared an unspoken bond. Bill would often write a tribute to special people. He shared his feelings about Lynn the week after her accident.

There is an often used saying that the good die young.

The Story of Lynn

Lynn Smith's tragic death in an automobile accident last week sadly reminds us that we sometime lose our best in their youth. Lynn was 19, had been a brilliant high school student and was enrolled at Lambuth College. The loss of such a person in a small town is far more than a loss to the family. It is the loss to the entire population. There is not one of us who had not been brightened by Lynn's cheerfulness. It wasn't always a spoken word from her...many times it was only a passing smile. She made us feel good with her presence, her youthful energy and the positive way she went about things. All of us profited from her very existence.

The frustration, helplessness and even the anger that rushes from our hearts as we stand by so incapable of understanding is unexplainable.

We tend to judge others and repeatedly ask why we are to lose someone like Lynn. One who has so much talent, so many things she was rushing to do. So much good to be done. So many people to be touched by this young student. We grope for the answer to these questions so much that it is easy for us to forget that no mater what our losses are... God doesn't make mistakes. All creatures and the things therein are God's..Lynn was his too!

~ The Jody Story

Jody was a young man that I watched grow up in our church. He and Nikki were to be married. Nikki's future mother-in-law brought her to our shop to find her a wedding dress. She was so tiny and we did not have any thing appropriate for her to wear. That evening, reflecting about some of the clothes that I still had of Lynn's. I remembered a dress that was in her collection that I thought it would be perfect for Nikki. It was white. It was appropriate. It was tiny.

After the wedding she returned the dress and I put it away with Lynn's other treasures.

Nikki was expecting their third child when Jody was killed in a plane crash. It was not instant, and she stayed by his side in the hospital while she was carrying Gracie. After Gracie was born, the dress reappeared in my mind and I thought " I must give it back to Nikki and maybe Gracie can wear it someday". Then I had a revelation. My sister, Sara, designs and sews heirloom clothing for infants and children. So I took the dress to her and said "Let's give Nikki the dress back in the form of a christening gown for Gracie." She created the most beautiful gown and embroidered Lynn's name and the date she wore the dress, Nikki and Jody's names and wedding date and Gracie's name and date of birth. Jody's mother wrote a poem for the christening ceremony. I feel that dress served several purposes. It was certainly healing for me.

The Story of Lynn

Life goes on. I had to deal with my situation. I did meet with one of the truck drivers. That did not help much, but it was something I had to do. I cried almost every night. I would wake in the middle of the night with tears on my pillow and not even know that I had been crying. Every morning, for at least a year, my first thought was Lynn. Then gradually, it would be a few seconds before my thoughts were about her. Each day became a little easier for me. Although I would still think about her every day, my life was not consumed with the accident. Now I needed a project.

Chapter Seven ~ Reality

How do I regroup? What about her clothes, her jewelry, her room, her friends? It was so much to deal with, but I tried to stay positive.

Our very dear friends Margaret and Benard embraced us with their love and also shared their lovely boat the *Aqua Mist*. We spent many healing days with them.

When the days seemed empty, my mind would reflect on the little journal of recipes that I had been collecting to give Lynn when she married. Then I began to write little stories and decided that I would type them and tie with ribbons and give to my friends for Christmas.

Well, the more I wrote, the bigger my idea grew. (God always knows what we need). It began to develop into a book. I called my sister Sara almost everyday to ask her what she thought about an idea or how I should do certain things. She was such a great help to me, My shoulder to lean on and my journalist to learn from. She also wrote the preface which captured Lynn's personality. *Roses In December* was bound in turquoise leather, with peach end paper. Lynn's two favorite colors. The title came from a meeting with the president of Lambuth University and a poem that he shared with us. The books were ordered and I gave them to my family and friends at a reception and book signing the following Christmas. To date I have given over 3500 books to friends and have shared them with people I did not know. Any proceeds from the book has benefited the *Lynn Smith Scholarship*. Although this was a new experience for me, it was truly a blessing as well as a challenge. It has been a way to share and keep Lynn's memory alive. This project helped me through many days and nights. The memorials that were sent after the accident established "The Lynn Smith Scholarship" We decided that we could do more to enhance the fund and began an annual "Lynn Smith Scholarship Dove Shoot". My father had the shoot for several years and Bob continued that tradition. Bob came up with the idea because it takes a good deal of time and money to prepare the fields for the shoot. The participants always asked to help with the expenses, we gave them the opportunity and to donate to the scholarship.

The first year we needed a large table for the food. My dear friend and carpenter, Danny, built a table that I had designed and we still use it for the food but mostly for the

The Story of Lynn

centerpieces. I skirted tables to the floor and painted canvas toppers with sun flowers. We cooked ribs and chicken and made it a party.

The invitation list grew each year. Then it really was about Lynn. It had to be special: the invitations, the food, the music and especially, the table decorations. I called my friend Sandy and the table decorations really got exciting.

One year she came late in the afternoon. Bob had worked all day preparing for the shoot. He was really tired. We asked him to cut a tree for us to be used as the centerpiece. He did not agree quickly, He had no idea how big or what our plans were but he did cut the tree. It was big. This project turned into quite a production. The tree was huge and had to be anchored from the top and bottom and of course we had to have lights on the tree. Of course, we did not stop at lights. We added sunflowers, crows, some of them swinging. Also pumpkins and gourds. Sandy and I still laugh that she did not know Bob was upset. I did.

The centerpiece was spectacular. The next day it all came together, and Bob was very pleased. Each year has become a challenge to outdo the year before. As one who thrives on a project, the "Dove Shoot" gave me something to look forward to each year and also to keep Lynn's memory alive. The scholarship has benefited students at both Lambuth University and Adamsville High School.

Chapter Eight ~ Tears

Somehow life goes on. I remember Bob saying he wanted the world to stop. It did not stop, but twenty-five years later I still get a note, a hug, an unexpected visit from one of her friends or just an" I have been thinking about you". Getting back into the real world was more challenging than I expected. You meet new people and one of the first things they ask is "Do you have children?"

What am I supposed to say? "Yes, but she was killed".... or "No, we don't, but"....... By the time I fumbled an answer, they would be upset that they had asked. Then they would apologize for asking and some even cried. I believe that it is alright to ask. Most of us still want to talk about our loved ones. Now I say "our only daughter was killed in a car accident when she was 19."

It is hard to control my tears. A song in church or a little note I find can bring the tears. Soon after the accident, Bob and I were in New York with a business associate and a gentlemen that we had just met. It was a fun restaurant and the waiters would burst into song when they took your order Our waiter sang "The Rose", which had been sung at Lynn's service. Bob and I both broke into tears.

We live in a broken world, and I know bad things happen to good people. I know that God is always with me and that he will never leave me. I also know that prayer is a must.

Psalm 30:5 says, *"Weeping may linger for the night but, joy comes with the morning. We have the assurance that God will wipe away every tear from our eyes and death and pain will be no more."*

Chapter Nine ~ Gods Comfort

It has been hard to go on living without her. I still feel so blessed to have been Lynn's mother for 19 years. I realize there are many parents that have their children for such a short time and struggle with horrible disease or injuries for a long time. I now believe there are things worse than death.

Lynn was such a joy to her father and me. She was an excellent student, ranked in the top ten of her graduating class, first chair flute, very independent and always, yes always on time.

I cannot imagine how I could have made it without my faith in God. He is a very present help, my refuge in times of trouble. God is my comfort.

Chapter Ten ~ The Hole in My Heart

Many years later, I still have a hole in my heart from the loss of my only child, Lynn. I do know that as time has passed, it has become smaller. There were many days when I could not find enough projects to keep me busy, while, other days found me not doing anything except enduring the grief and physical pain that I felt.

I miss her so much, but life is a journey and I am moving on. The bad memories fade and the good memories get brighter. Through all the pain and grief, I know that God has given me all that I need to help fill the hole in my heart.

I have so many precious children, old friends and new that have become so important to this process.

My sister Sara and brother- in- law Mike have shared their son Stephen and daughter Elizabeth with me. When Stephen was born and I saw him for the first time, I did not know that he was not mine and I still don't. He has been so much fun for Bob and me to watch become a young man. Now that he is married, I have two more loves, Donna, his wife and a precious little girl named Millie.

Elizabeth has been my other little girl. When I first saw her I thought, "I have seen that face before." I came home and found my baby picture, and she looked just like me. She and Sara and Mike and Stephen lived with us for a few months when she was two years old. She was a delight. She slept with us almost every night. Later she would call us and say "Names Lizabeth." When she would hang up she would say "Luv." She still does. She is married to Ryan, and now I have Holt, Lacey Claire and Colby Jane that I adore. They love us and bring us so much joy

I have other nieces and nephews B.K., Cole, Jennifer, Page and Kyle, Austen and Ashley. Also, Rachael, Lauren, Jason, Christopher, McLain and Irby. Since they do not live near us, I do not get to spend as much time with them, but they have given us much pleasure through the years. We lost our precious Christopher in 2011 in a car accident.

Ben and Katherine, the children of our friends Margaret and Benard, have been like our own children. We have spent almost every Christmas, Thanksgiving, Easter, Mothers Day and many family vacations with them. Ben called me "Frisha" for years, and now Katherine has married Eric and

The Story of Lynn

that is one more to love. I get a lot of love and hugs from them. Now we have their son Boone.

Anna, our exchange student, came to visit the first year after Lynn's accident and has been to visit many times. She has two precious boys, Carl-Johan and Edward Robert. They are a part of our family and have brought us much happiness. Anna has kept Lynn's memory alive for her children to know about her.

The four Pettits, John Mark, Ali, Andrew and Laura Dee. They are so special to us. We get double love and hugs from all of them. They call often and come to hunt and fish on our farm.

I loved Angela from the start. She married Kacy, the son of my best friend since childhood, Kaye. We planned their wedding for a year and shared a lot of precious moments together. We have shared several vacations. Now I have Angela and Kacy's daughter, Hannah to love.

Bob and I have friends that certainly have been a part of our healing process. Suzanne and Ancil, Jack and Insa, David and Anita and Jimmy and Bonita. We celebrated the Millennium and have enjoyed the Grove Park Inn, Blackberry farm, Boston, Canada, garden shows and danced the night away. We still look forward to the next celebration.

I have a group of friends that meet each Tuesday for fun and fellowship. Nancy, is a friend from childhood; Suzanne,

Sara, Lee, Sharon, Bettye, Mary Ann, Patricia R and Dot are also a part of this group. These women are a strong force in my life. A diverse group, they are smart and strong, teachers and listeners, and all around happy people. We share and learn from each other.

Then there is my friend Sandy. We decorate our houses, discuss our tablescapes, menus, and even decide on paint colors by phone. We talk at least weekly. She makes me laugh. Bob always knows when I am talking with her because I am laughing.

Becky is my prayer warrior. She was my next door neighbor for several years. She was there when Lynn started first grade. Becky's was the first written note I received after Lynn's accident. I have received many notes from her through the years, and we have shared many phone conversations. I cherish our friendship.

My friend Danny is a talent, so blessed with skills beyond belief. We built a house from the ground up with no real blueprints. Just a dream in my head and some computer drawings. It was a wonderful project, and I spent endless hours designing and planning. If I could think of how I wanted it to be, then Danny could build it. I said many times over the five years that we built, that I spent more time with him than I did Bob. Danny has been an amazing friend and a great source of help to me during the healing process.

The Story of Lynn

Our canasta group meets each third Monday night and we have for 50 years. Margaret, Pam, Carol Jane, Neita, Anita, Kaye and Gwen. What a support group! We lost Gwen to cancer in 2009.

My mother and father gave me more love than I could ever deserve. My mother taught me the joys of being a homemaker. My father died a few years ago and his life could be my next book. Before he died, he was always there for me. He showed me how to appreciate and live in today. He helped me to understand the love of our Heavenly Father.

There are so many people who have touched my life, and I know that each one has had an effect on the hole in my heart and my healing process. I know that I can never be a "10", but with all the love of these young people and my family and friends, and God's guidance, I am trying to be the best "9" that I can be.

Chapter Eleven ~ Years Later

I still feel her presence when I look at a picture she painted for me that hangs over my computer. I still see her bony little fingers as she played her flute. I still smell her hair when it was freshly washed. I still hear her subtle whistle when she came home from school. I still miss her.

In Lynn's high school yearbook her saying was "Live for today, dream for tomorrow and learn from yesterday." I reflect on her dreams and I do think about what would she have become. Would she have married? Would I have been a grandmother? Where would she have lived? Shawn, her dear friend and mine, was reflecting one day about Lynn, (she referred to him as her "brother by a different mother" and he had the same feelings. What would she have become? I do wonder.

Sunsets are more important to me now. Each time I gaze at a sunset, I marvel at Gods wonderful creations. I always smile, and sometimes I shed a tear and I know that God has a very special assistant named Lynn in charge of sunsets.

Each time you see a sunset, my prayer for you is that you will be reminded of your precious memories. Perhaps you will think of Lynn. I hope that you will marvel at God's wondrous creations. I trust that you will feel His presence and remember that He promised that He will never leave us nor forsake us.

This one thing I know, Lynn believed in God; she was happy, and she lived her life to the fullest. Lynn is at peace. I am at peace. I feel so blessed that God chose me to be Lynn's Mother.

Acknowledgements

I thank my husband Bob, for his love and support in sharing the loss of our daughter, Lynn. To my family, especially my sister Sara, who has been my biggest supporter in writing this book. I know they all loved Lynn dearly. To our friends Margaret and Benard for always being there and allowing us to heal in the warmth of southern winters, to my canasta friends, Kaye, Margaret, Carol Jane, Neita, Anita and Pam for the Monday nights that I cried and they silently knew why; and to my friend Sandy who makes me laugh and shares Lynn's birthday, and to Lynn's friends who still treasure her memory. I have to express my gratitude to Mary Ann. You have been an inspiration and have provided so much helpful information.

To God be the glory, He is constant with me and has been every day through this journey. He has pulled me through when I did not think I could make it and has enabled me to live with my loss.

> # LYNN
> *"The Refreshing One"*
> He who believes in Me, just as the scripture says,
> streams of living water will flow
> from his inner-most being.
>
> John 7:38

The above was written on a plaque given to Lynn as a graduation present. and it hangs in my office today under her picture. It gives me the best description of what Lynn was to me as her father.

She brought nothing but joy to her mother and me- whether it was through her love and respect for us, through her friends, through her achievements, or just her outlook on life that was always expressed by a subtle little whistle.

Through her spirit she took the worst of things and made them better, and she took the best of things and made them super. God would share it with one of us, and we would share it with each other. She had the knowledge and wisdom to understand things beyond her years, and we learned about the joy of living and love as a family on a daily basis.

She had an uncanny desire to plan ahead, to achieve, and to do things on a timely basis. She always remembered important dates weeks ahead. She had a calendar on her wall with dates a year in advance. She would always prompt me as much as an hour before a ballgame started, and I would say "Lynn, the game doesn't start until 7:00, and she would say,

"But Dad, they run out at 20 'til'."

She was living proof of God's promise: For God giveth to a man that is good in his sight wisdom, and knowledge, and joy; Ecclesiastes 2:26

And as God said: There is a right time for everything: A time to be born, and a time to die; Ecclesiastes 3:1.

I know Lynn was prepared and on time December 18. 1984, at 2:32 pm, when she met her Lord and Savior, Jesus Christ, who gave her the promise: And whosever liveth and believeth in Me shall never die. John 11:26.

I love her very much and thank God every day for the memories we made together.

Her Dad
1985

reprinted from the book *Roses in December*

Epilogue

On the anniversary of Lynn's accident, her friend Tammy posted on face book page her memories of Lynn. It made me happy and sad to read the post and the memories of the others who responded.

~ Tammy

Do you know what you were doing on this day 24 years ago? I remember just like it was yesterday. I was wrapping a microwave for my grandparents for Christmas. Mom and Ms Linda Freeman were shampooing the carpets in our Tanyard house. The phone rang to give me the most devastating news I had ever heard. My best and most precious friend Lynn Smith had been killed in a wreck on her way home from Lambuth!! I remember all the emotions running from you are joking to no that is not possible.

This is a day I always reflect, cry and laugh hysterically as I remember Lynn. I can see us fighting over a green crayon. I see us on vacation wherever our parents dragged us at the time and the memories just go on and on. But can you not her say..."Good Grief"...and she would take off with red pumps blazing to correct a wrong or set someone straight!!

Every time I hear Silent Night I think of Stace and Shane playing their trumpets at the cemetery on that cold December day. It always brings a tear to my eye. I thank God for the time that we all had her in our lives.

I love you all my friends.

~ Response by Lanetta

Tammy

This day is always very sad for me too. I think of Lynn many, many times throughout the year, sometimes at the oddest moments. I saw a Dart company truck the other day and thought of the funny red Dart cap she wore for a while. Every time I see a neat window display, I think of her and her creative bent and sense of style. Anna Grace plays flute and every band concert makes me think of her! I saw a piccolo soloist the other day and I can just hear Lynn reaching for those high notes. I saw parts of "Your a Good Man, Charlie Brown" and I can't hear the Lucy speech without thinking of Lynn! She continues to live on in all of us because she made an impact on everyone she knew. I miss her still...

~ Terri P

Tammy. thanks for posting this note. I think it is so important for those that are no longer with us to (be) remembered on this day as well as other days. I was thinking about her last month-she just popped into my head. Her and her parents. I am sure something triggered the thought, but I cannot recall what it was. Thanks for sharing.

~ Scott

"Sad Day"

"in the past several years it's become so hard to imagine that lynn has been gone longer than she was with us.. I think of her all the time.. there was so much life bundled up in that tiny little package, all that beautiful spirit and energy had no choice but to live on and on in our hearts.. every year in this day i take a little time just for remembering lynn.. as the years have passed the sheer pain and anger of losing her have certainly eased.. luckily, the painful part has been replaced with a comfort that comes from realizing how very lucky I was to have had even a minute with her. I was always drawn to lynn because of her fearless individuality.. she was always her own unique self, but in a way that never threatened anyone else's sensibilities..she was just lynn! she inspired me from the start to be myself no matter what..i remember playdates at their little house in dickey woods where lynn and i rocked out to 3 Dog Night! we were maybe all of 6 years old, but we knew all the words to "eli's coming"..i still have no idea what that song was about, but it's our song! i remember looong talks about life and hopes and dreams while we were locked inside "ma mil's store

doing the windows. one of my most-prized possessions is a photograph of me and lynn and santa claus when we were 3 years old at the Christmas belle and beau pagent..we won, of course! haha...we got to wear crowns! i'm reminded of lynn by so many things, and visit some awesome memories very often..mostly, i'm so very thankful to lynn..i know that my life would not have been what it has been without the inspiration and confidence that she gave me..i'm so glad i took the time to tell here while she was here..i've been very lucky to work in fashion and travel the world and have so many experiences that i know lynn would have loved..and i believe with all my heart that she's been with me every step of the way..

ilove her and i miss her all the time!

xxxs

~ Stace

Tammy, what a wonderful tribute. I've spent the last few hours reading every post on this thread and thinking back on days gone by...Lynn holds a special place in all our hearts. The one comfort I have found over the years is this: we will see her again one day. Until then, sleep in heavenly peace my dear friend.

CPSIA information can be obtained at www.ICGtesting.com
Printed in the USA
LVOW041026171112

307702LV00003B/5/P